NEW
AND
SELECTED
POEMS

NEW
AND
SELECTED
POEMS

James Schevill

Swallow Press/Ohio University Press

Athens

Swallow Press/Ohio University Press, Athens, Ohio 45701
© 2000 by James Schevill
Printed in the United States of America
All rights reserved. Published 2000

Swallow Press/Ohio University Press books
are printed on acid-free paper ⊗™

09 08 07 06 05 04 03 02 01 00   5 4 3 2 1

Library of Congress Cataloging-in-Publication Data
Schevill, James Erwin, 1920–
  [Poems Selections]
  New and selected poems / James Schevill.
      p. cm.
    ISBN 0-8040-1027-7 (alk. paper) — ISBN 0-8040-1028-5
(pbk. : alk paper)
      I. Title.

PS3537.C3278 N4 2000
811'.54—dc21
                              00-041013

Acknowledgments

Many of the poems in the *New Poems* section appeared first in the following magazines and pamphlets: *The Michigan Quarterly*, *Talisman*, *ESP*, *The Pearl River Review*, *West Branch*, and *James Schevill: A Sampler of His Poems* published by Don Emblen, The Clamshell Press, Santa Rosa, California.

I would like to thank David Sanders, the director of Swallow Press/Ohio University Press, for his editorial advice in the selection of poems for this book. Also, I would like to thank my friends Ferol Egan, Robert Peterson, Stanley Noyes, and Edwin Honig for their help.

to Margot

Contents

New Poems

Wildfire Vision   3

Nevada Bus Encounter   5

The Last Decade of de Kooning's Paintings   6

The Pale Man: Joseph Cornell   7

Kafka in Prague   9

Master of the Colloquial   12

Seeing the Wind   13

The Memory of It   14

The Continuous River   15

Threat of Invisible Wind-Voices   16

Race Car Driver   17

Playground Pickup Game in the Time of
    Millionaire Basketball Players   19

A Jazz Master Improvising   21

Quixote Visions   22

The Rembrandt Confrontation   27

Selected Poems

From *Private Dooms and Public Destinations:*
    Poems 1945–1962

The Will of Writing   45

In the Peaceable Kingdom a Man Sings of Love   46

Funeral   47

A Plea for Alias   48

A Guilty Father to His Daughter   49

Death of a Cat   50

Neighbors   52

The Momentary Glimpses of Women
    through Windows   54

The Rake's Resentment of Verdi's *Falstaff*   55

The Descent: Hotel Biron (The Rodin Museum)   56

Stories of the Soviet Union: June 1961   58

From Sword, Sex, and God's Word
    at the Philosopher's Gate   64

From *The Stalingrad Elegies* (1964)

    The Piano on the Street   73

    The Snow Woman   76

    The Wound of Flatness   77

From *Violence and Glory: Poems 1962–1968*

    Withered Daffodils   81

    London Pavement Artist   82

    After the Objects, a Subject   83

    The Clear Angels of Dawn in the Country   84

From *Ambiguous Dancers of Fame* (1987)

Mexican Flower Arrangement   87

The Dreamer of Light Sings His Song of Sounds   88

Roadblock   89

Neighboring Walls   90

The Writer and the Gardener   91

The Gardener's Celebration   92

The First Heavy Rain of the Rainy Season   93

Dog-Pack   94

Frank Lloyd Wright Desperately Designing a Chair   95

The Oedipus Scream of Olivier   96

All Day Driving across Kansas   97

Love Song in Summer's Furnace Heat   98

From *The Complete American Fantasies* (1996)

Always We Walk through Unknown People   101

The Country Fair of Childhood   102

Hats and Ears for Charles Ives   103

Wallace Stevens at Ease with Marble Cake   106

The Peaceable Kingdom of Edward Hicks   107

Mr. and Mrs. Herman Melville at Home,
    Isolated in Their Rooms   108

Huck Finn at Ninety, Dying in
    a Chicago Boardinghouse Room   109

Bashir Was My Name   110

On the Burning of Mingus's Bass   112

What Are the Most Unusual Things
    You Find in Garbage Cans?   113

Kristallnacht   118

Green Frog at Roadstead, Wisconsin   120

Love, Do Not Shun the Dark Gargoyle   121

The Mathematician Thinking of Ghost Numbers   122

On the Beach Watched by a Sea Gull   123

A Screamer Discusses Methods of Screaming   124

Street Corner Signals   125

William Carlos Williams and T. S. Eliot
    Dancing over London Bridge in the Arizona
    Desert at Lake Havasu   126

NEW

POEMS

Wildfire Vision

All my life I've lived on fire's edge.
Three years old, I was carried away
from Berkeley's wildfire of 1923,
our house barely saved from surging flames.
In my teens, shocked suddenly awake,
crying "Smoke! I smell smoke!"
I watched, dazed, as Father in pajamas
fought flames valiantly with a thin, green
garden hose until, mercifully, goliath firemen
with coiling, heavy hoses, cascaded water mercilessly,
drenching Father's library into stinking pages.

Back in Berkeley, in 1991, I witnessed
a black, demonic cloud cover dry hills
and prepared to evacuate reliving memory.
What to rescue? Friends' lifetime possessions
vanished in the fury of wildfire,
but our neighborhood was spared.
Now when summer dries the hills brown again
and I hear sirens howl their warning,
I feel the hills wait tensely for fog's advance.
Yet I'm not surprised when one wildfire survivor
says, "I needed a fire. I needed an excuse to start over."

Tell me, my city, why do you attract fire?
A man or woman moves through life
like a pillar of fire in furious cars,
challenging us to follow, pray, or jeer.

Flames of responsibility puzzle the crowd.
Factories we turned into temples of fire.
Claimed Henry Ford: "The man who
builds a factory builds a temple.
The man who works there worships there."
Wildfire is the secret dream within our eyes.

Fire of desire is my indulgent sweet
fire of despair the vice I suffer.
But if I love through fantasy of fire
and lose through greed of fire,
I live with fire's losses. I dream of
Asian countries where an oil lamp
marks the site of death, flickering flame
signifying the lost spirit shining
free on its journey to eternity.
Wildfire is the secret dream within my eyes.

Every bright blaze attracts.
I pause to read its illumination.
Soon all is ashes and I regret
living between explosive action and troubled sleep.
Fire makes possible the search for balance.

Writing is a hand moving in fire,
shaping resurrection rage.
My burning words, my self
born again in lucid flame words,
rises from the ashes of death
creating heat essential to birth,
wildfire cleansing the mind's wilderness.

Nevada Bus Encounter

Past shacks shredded like snakeskins,
lost gas stations slumped in car-wreck dumps,
the bus limps, smoking to legendary casinos.
The young European professor, speaking
precise English with British accent,
talks casually to the fat lady beside him,
measuring her huge self, her quick humor
smiling through wrinkles around her puzzling eyes,
heavily powdered face, fancy red fingernails.
Politely, he asks what she does. Tearing off
a piece of newspaper spread across her enormous lap,
she scribbles, holds it to his eyes: *Whore.*

Treeless mountains on the horizon
brood, isolated, bare in volcanic heaves.

The Last Decade of de Kooning's Paintings

With Alzheimer's coming on,
struggle to do what you cannot do.

No more personal conflicts of representation
as in the sensual, distorted *Woman* series.

Now paint the simple surface, gliding color,
design lovely curves, no longer explorer of depth.

Act out, renew an elemental state of being.
Assistants prepare huge canvases and you stand there:

I can still paint, I am desperate for simplicity.
I will find bright, primary colors like Matisse's endgame.

Simplicity picks out brush-lines one by one,
spinning loss into a fiery, brightly colored spiderweb.

See, I am trying to paint a radiance
beyond painting, design against death!

If depth of art is a lost beacon, look!
Radiant end-lines appear, dark end's eclipse!

The Pale Man: Joseph Cornell

He was so pale his skin faded into invisibility
like white ripples of sand in a desert.
"Shy" doesn't fit him; "absent" is wrong.
Visitors looked at him as though an appearance
was somehow strangely part of a disappearance,
a curious transparency of presence
as if surreal vision created billowing ghost flesh.

Always he dressed in grays and blacks.
Even in spring and summer when the world
bloomed in color, he seemed to live
in black and white; sometimes he'd wear
a brown sweater like a colorless beetle.
He ate more sweets than he did food,
and he chewed with tiny, quick bites
quivering like a bird nervous to be watched.
Very thin, he wore his clothes very large,
and he walked kind of lost in his pants.

All of his life he lived in Flushing, Long Island,
in a small, conventional house on Utopia Parkway,
with his mother and invalid brother till they died;
then he lived alone with paradoxical Utopian eyes
searching to create collaged museum boxes,
which he eyed as minimal, rectangular containers
to transform clandestine images bought from souvenir shops,
flea markets, and used bookstores with back number magazines:
a maestro of American waste who knew the combinations of
   magic.

He loved the old, radiant performers; their fading photos
haunted his boxes, starlight caught in proscenium pride.
Sharpening surrealism with American pragmatism,
he explored any unusual found transformation:
Woolworth necklaces, stuffed birds, pharmacy bottles,
toys and games, soap bubbles, pipes, maps,
a new wild geography of imagination.
Once he took pears and put nails in them as if
metallic force could make fragile beauty endure.
He connected farapart images with faraway lives
and linked the stubborn fantasies of his rooted life
to the reality of visions that Americans need.

In a dark time of depression and wars,
his pale face stared into infinity's wonderland.

Kafka in Prague

I

The great river in my city flowed through
fantastic architecture, fusing Gothic and Baroque together.
On the river, white swans arching their necks
were the only measure of tranquillity
as I watched every day the current
writhing under the ancient, prideful bridgeheads
like the syllables of compulsive language.

So I came to language like an old boatsman
embarking on a journey through ruined civilizations,
compelled to search for a special sound—
struggling to simplify my tangled German syntax
through dominant, buzzing Czech—
chained to my father and mother
like a sawblade to twin sawblades,
agonizing all my fantasies of sex
through whores and victims I called fiancées,
hoping blindly freedom is possible
if that impossible word can be found.

II

Through a jagged confusion of beautiful architecture
and modern stopgap, surrealistic time,
I stare always into a dark, confined room,
condemned to spy on my parents' intimacy:

"Did I ever tell you that I admire my father,
 you know that he is my enemy!"—
My stern father struggling to commercial success,
and my mother who sacrifices herself blindly
for what she calls desperately—the family life—
(We are frozen together in one grave site
in the New Jewish cemetery, my name
finally above my parents' on the tombstone) . . .

III

Time still burrows into my bureaucratic eye
as I work daily with insurance statistics,
an official compromising with other servile officials,
condemned to deal with a statistical age,
numbers defining the fear of mortality.

After work, striding through river shadows
up to Hradcany Castle to my little writing room,
I still write my lost German in a Czech-speaking city,
seeking ambiguous, simple sentences that shape
the planes of paradox and define
the impersonal bureaucracy that will rule the future.

I write to explore the jagged edge
of language that catches, laughing,
on the sharply detailed mystery of things,
a time when I walk daily
through the nightmare of reality
between real castles and trials,
bear witness to a false aristocracy
savaged by a people's revolution,

people transforming horribly into insects,
their faces illuminated
in grotesquely comic smiles.

IV

At night, unable to sleep,
loving and chastising my fiancée
across the savage necessity of distance,
I write to her with defensive half-truths:
"Simply rush through the nights forever writing,
that is what I want. To go to hell because of it,
or go mad, that too is what I want because
it is the inevitable, foreshadowed consequence."

A curious, lifeless fame looms beyond the grave.
I do not want it! Burn my books and manuscripts!
My scraped bare, homeless language
echoes back my comic, infernal words
dancing through the ancient clash
of brilliant architecture in my mind.

Master of the Colloquial

in memoriam: William Stafford 1914–1993

If the necessity of
colloquial language
nags at the poet,
how does the
relevant word—
(Mr. Relevant, Bill!)—
pierce through the
channels of confusion
and create the right tone?
How can the commonplace
renew the sacred mystery?

A huge country
with gaping mouth
seeking to absorb
many languages
into one American tongue—
how can a flood-torn
midwestern cornfield
speak the syllables of
an urban skyscraper?

To be "the slow guest
of the world," to connect
things with patient
gesture, to listen
and not just be, to find,
the infinitive is the world,
to listen is to see.

Seeing the Wind

Often in summer woods
nothing moves;
staring I see
the illusion of silence.

The first motion is a dancing leaf,
followed by a million flutterers.
Suddenly, the sky erupts
with savage clouds!
Branches wave
with mad signals,
their arms jingling leaf-bell music!

How wicked and joyous the wind we cannot see—
How wonderful the wild masks of invisibility!

The Memory of It

Mind going, memory flutters like a fragile fish
striking frantically for points of contact where it happened,
or it did not happen. Fading into the unknown
it is a giant question mark, a lost oasis of time.

Yet, suddenly, she begins to play the piano
and remembers it perfectly, playing with
absolute precision, it flows with supreme melodies,
dynamics of passion, phrases of perfection.

If it disappears again, and the fluttering fish
of failing memory strikes again, the hidden channel of it
remains; approaching night can never forget
the time of it playing its supreme music.

The Continuous River

in memory of M. L. *Rosenthal*

If the search for art is light
     out of darkness,
death is not the art of flight,
     recovery of night.

Death is the art of conclusion,
     a final fusion
when the eyes of doubt close
     and the continuous river flows.

Threat of Invisible Wind-Voices

At night in Los Alamos, Mexican colonial town,
my wife and I look up at the Baroque
church facade soaring eerily in moonlight.
Below us, plodding around the square,
a stooped policeman sags under a bright
red cloth wrapped tightly around his head.

"Mister policeman," my wife calls down.
"Why are you wearing that lovely cloth?"
"For my ears," he answers, "to keep them warm,
hidden from cold, invisible wind-voices."

He slumps along on his tour of the square.
Silent, the night hangs brooding warmly in
menacing vacuum over the desert's dry, oceanic
calm as I listen tensely for cold, invisible wind-voices.

Race Car Driver

We all come from small towns
looking for big victories.
We're all looking for a buddy system,
but I got no buddies.

It's wound up in the way you attack.
Sometimes I get stuck back there with guys
and I have to jam it and make
some moves I'm not thrilled about.
It gets too tight, aiming between cars,
aiming to make it three-wide
and stay in the middle of things.

We go a-bumping and a-slamming
and a-bumping and a-slamming.
I like the preferred line, the bottom groove,
and that's the right way to go.

All day long, the roar haunts your ears.
You're always asking how can I
take a car out from between one of us
or move him from the outside lane
to the inside lane? If the black car

keeps coming and coming, on the last lap
that's not the kind of black you want to see.
But I'm pretty strong off the corners.
He might get under me,

but I keep him off up high and he
just can't get down there.
He keeps struggling to set me up
every lap trying to get by me,
and I really think he's going to get me.

When I cross the finish line,
he drives up and gives me a love tap.
He drives into the side of me and just waves.

Playground Pickup Game in the Time of Millionaire Basketball Players

Evenings, lagging on my way home,
I stop in the park to watch
the daily pickup basketball game.
Fifty years ago I too played every afternoon,
practicing cloudbusters from what is now
three-point range, exulting in a stark two points,
while dreaming of the triple in a future fantasy.

Every afternoon pickup players gather,
mostly black, old, young, fat, lean,
a few white and Asian contenders
yearning to be point guards with their speedy dribble.
The players rap in rhythmical sequence as they play,
a second game of prodding words:
"You guys run so fast
the ground feels sorry for you!"

Now it's a defensive war
beating your man off the dribble,
exhausting him with head fakes and eye fakes,
running the pick and roll to
finger lift lightly into the net.

Play hard means drive like a demon,
the defense smothering you in a
military blockade, knocking people,
getting a good hand on elusive bodies.

Twilight reveals a game for eager drivers,
fanatic fans, all those who soar for the basket
knowing through the net, aloof, evasive,
sounds the mocking swish of time and money.

A Jazz Master Improvising

"It's the ultimate intellectual achievement.
And when there's emotion behind it, it's sublime."

Branford Marsalis

Last night I heard the sound return like a river
searching for oceanic freedom.
Improvisation demands a *now* quality
haunted by our past masters' intelligence.

When I'm into it, it's me playing
suddenly, exploring all complexities,
melody so high I'm singing cloud to lightning:
Behind me I feel the solid *clunk* of earth harmonies,
syncopated rhythms pricking my skin, driving up to
pillars of ecstasy, choking my throat with high cadence. . . .
Failing is like falling down an elevator shaft.

Think of everyone outside who tries to improvise fame,
dealing money, sex, glamorous cars like glory,
but the true improviser plays with different honor,
merging emotion with intellect, then it's sublime.

In the dark an intense, massive structure moves,
a burning joy clarifies the flesh of grief.

Quixote Visions

to the memory of Rudolph Schevill

(1)

Magic shines a voice,
spears of sound in the burning landscape,
desert shimmering with heat wave light
to polish my lucid tones of invention.
What I shape is the weather of identity.

(2)

To speak of identity as weather
is to forsake comfortable souls
for the spirit's saddle of leather.

(3)

People walk in my lost footsteps,
soar on words of my fantasies.
Sweet sounds of chivalric hope
flow into the dreamer's trap
where false manners
            teach us how to sleep.

(4)

Loom proud, crazy, erotic,
you begin to be quixotic.

(5)

To earn the clown as servant
become a master of comedy.
With a fanatic's deft finesse
dance the grotesque dream,
pleasure has a light step.

(6)

When the clown perceives you,
practise your sober reply,
knowing solemnity is never true.

(7)

Come with me, Sancho,
leave your wife and children.
In the blinking of your eye
an island shines in space.
From servant you ascend to governor,
your skeptic's look a ruler's face.

(8)

I give you your island, Sancho,
cleanse it of evil, pronounce
judgment on its citizens' vices;
if power is too complex for simplicity
on your ass, Dapple, ride back to liberty.

(9)

Horse and ass, we rode together,
Sancho—animals teach men
loyalty—to carry the weight
of time, patience of animal fate.

(10)

To see an army in a flock of sheep
was my message. Is it so strange?
Armies are defenders that attack.

(11)

Sancho doubts everything.
    I praise every thing.
        Between doubt and praise
            dreams begin to sing.

(12)

A chamberpot for a helmet.
If only warriors
                had a sense of humor.

(13)

Honey is not for the ass's mouth,
says Sancho—yet on a sweet tongue
words writhe sweetly and sound wrong.

(14)

Soft words make soft survival.
Hard words harden into time
where only floating legends
sing forever without rival.

(15)

Dulcinea—name of sweet ambitions.
Love is more than touch.
Who sees feminine grace
sleeps with spiritual decisions.

(16)

When ambition falls away
find the simple air.
For one second, love and freedom
shine in a single stare.

(17)

To love is to sacrifice, to ride
against windmills, to put on lost armor.
If a woman has no name, no figure,
            no glittering eye to defend,
why create false wars
            when there are lips to kiss?

(18)

For love to cross every frontier,
I trusted armor, armor is false.
Trust men and women naked
in their primal loving pulse.

(19)

Farewell . . . From every journey knowledge.
To those who stay at home
                  may their roots prosper.
May the roots dream,
                  the voyagers return safely
when they've cleansed themselves
                  of the glowing myths.

The Rembrandt Confrontation

To Henk and Elizabeth Meijer and Nathan Oliveira

*(1) In Amsterdam, an American Artist
Visits the Grave of Saskia Rembrandt*

In the Old Church, stones break,
    death, in bony time, under the floor.
Over the heaving, cracked floor I stumble.
      On her grave no name,
      no Saskia, no love-memory,
      only time's ingathering flow
      over the cold stone.

Born American, how can I paint
    lost, fragmented forms of history?
In a time of instant confusion
      I travel to Amsterdam to confront
      Rembrandt, the greatest history painter;
      to seek in his paintings the visionary space
      an artist can find only in his masters.

Saskia is his vision, Saskia lost;
    how he painted her as Flora,
goddess of springtime flowers,
      gown of lavish green,
      hair and staff all garlanded,
      mouth sensuous with desire. . . .
      The painting lives in Russia, in the Hermitage.

At the Metropolitan in New York, I visited often
    Rembrandt's curious painting

of Saskia as Bellona, hesitant war goddess,
    sword arm dangling as she conquers
    seemingly unable to perform a warlike act.
    Underneath, as x-rays prove, he painted Saskia
    naked, symbolic war covering love's wonder.

Old Church, Old Church of death,
where is the wonder of eternal love?

(2) *Rembrandt: Self-Portrait, 1628—22 Years Old*

"Guess me, young forever,
    I am not your Rembrandt.
My curly, wild hair dazzles
    with eternal youth
that feels but cannot know
    what it desires,
hypnotized in lily-pad dreams
    on clamorous Amsterdam canals
where youth renews forever
    spring's quickening flower-time.

"Without fresh, young faces of desire
    art has no history;
the tiny rose tucked in my ear
    asserts my flowering.
My proud eyes stare from the dark
    blessing the challenge of light!
My pure desire of sexual union
    breaks out of death's shadow,
joining light, the lovely intruder,
    in battle against dark time."

(3) The Painting of History

In Rembrandt's time, dramatic action
soared from the Bible, sacred subjects
for the painter, resurrection,
    lust of sainthood;
the painter as Master of Revelation—
    portraiture a lesser art—
huge canvases depicting moral acts
    to justify man's Godhead!

Today we painters paint God into invisibility. We search for abstract, brilliant myths of transformation with bold colors clashing like gates in infinite space. Seeking extensions of space that transfigure the sky daily, we suspend on canvas huge, thrusting images in distant time. We probe chaotic forms like mathematicians struggling to prove that enigmatic order exists even in whirling chaos!

I am such a painter driven to big canvases which only museums, alas, have walls big enough to display—epic space voyages in multi-layered, fever-dripping colors. Like Rembrandt, I married twice, painted those marriages with joy of naked flesh, and lost those women because I could not give to match their giving. My only gift is to my painting, the cursed dedication of art.

How different is my life from Rembrandt's. My painting slashes out of poverty's disorder, my childhood spent in a New York ghetto where my silent parents confronted each day grimly through trapped eyes and tense mouths, unable to release forgiving words against the long hours of factory work and paralyzing boredom shrouding their lives.

Against poverty and stifled parents, I could summon only a tormented will to draw frantic movements of escape. Fleeing ghetto vision and slave labor, at eighteen I enlisted in the Vietnam Adventure as it was called. I marched into the nightmare language of body counts, gooks, defoliation, jungle rot, language bleeding into scabs of meaning.

Into confinement of "Strategic Hamlets," we herded natives we could not understand, forcing them away from their homes. We planned endless air strikes on burning jungles we poisoned with Agent Orange, not realizing we poisoned ourselves. Trapped in the geography of hell, we experimented with the insane future of "computerized battlefields."

Invisible, "the gooks" tunneled under our thick-headed invasion, our know-nothing language where military jargon created its own invisible target of victory. At home, the country was ripped apart by splintered youth whom I joined after my discharge, my defiant long hair flowing demonically at countless demonstrations against the war's televised distance.

My gods became the visual revolutionary spirits. I traveled, smoking dope, hitching my way, from gallery to museum staring at Pollock, Still, Rothko, Diebenkorn, prime spirits of artistic revolt who helped me learn how to paint inside of my struggling outsider's life. Layering paint thick, violent on canvas, I accused:

> "Why am I condemned to paint war's insane fury?"
> Searching for a quiet, perceptive eye in today's whirlwind
>   of war,
> I stand in the Rijks Museum watching tourists gape
> at Rembrandt's freshly cleaned *The Night Watch*.

Preening in archaic uniforms, staring proudly across
the centuries, the guardsmen challenge each observer:
"Can you look at our communal band without searching
for some lost unity deep within your lonely self?"

How can I paint such radiant ghost-possession?
I dream of Rembrandt as some dead shaman
in his peculiar costumes, staring enigmatically
at me, asking, "Guess me, greet me if you can!"

(4) *Rembrandt: Self-Portrait, 1648—42 Years Old*

"See how we wealthy
    household masters
        command the clarity of good clothes.

"Rebellion here is
    sentenced to the confinement
        of prosperous illusion.

"I never lie in portraits,
    present this satire in a mirror,
        the mask of success,

"preening before my wife
    as Master of Art
        in darkening resolve.

"Light burns away
    all final questions;
        living with false fantasies,

"with teasing layers of torment
when we put on fancy clothes
to conceal naked dreams."

(5) *Wandering through Amsterdam*

In gray skies over Amsterdam, a city always light-torn,
        I see Rembrandt's obsession: streaks of sunlight
burst out of blackness illuminating rare earth-colors
                merging in the apocalyptic sequence of sunset to
                sunrise,
the historical painter's vision of death and resurrection.
                Visiting Rembrandt's house, I find him
vanished in history; only mocking tributes here,
                ghosts buried under memories of recent horror,
Jews deported from this neighborhood by the Nazis,
                Anne Frank and her family hidden in vanishing hope
amidst her dreams of movie stars she pinned on her hiding-
        place wall.
                Leaving Rembrandt's house, I walk the gray streets
of Amsterdam, gray men and gray women passing by
                absorbed in the rituals of universal urban problems:

Gray Man

Gray Man is almost invisible. He's there daily, creating routine
actions, but you don't see him. I paint him into abstraction.
Dressed in his gray clothes, he fades into crowds like an automa-
ton. His glasses glitter a little concealing his sight. Everything
he does is a truthful lie. He walks in daily paradox like an un-
dercover preacher. He believes that if God exists, justice will
prevail, although it may take eternal time. What Gray Man
knows can never be revealed. It will be acted out invisibly.

Gray Woman

I see her only in a blur. When she walks by, I never whistle. I
paint her twisted, in De Kooning shapes. Gray Woman wears
nondescript clothes and glasses like Gray Man, but her nature
is more explosive. Her ancestors are fire and storm. What she
knows, no one else knows. Her mind resists painting, full of
secrecy like a deep, endless mineshaft.

After the Second World War in the century of expanding
    technological wars, American painting seemed for the
        first time
to influence the world, compulsive energy of action painting
    spattering, dripping on canvases everywhere.
Behold the violent triumph of American Power!
    Dark, exuberant Saturn soars to the moon conquering
        space!
Star Wars! Precise, pinpoint rockets as eagles of
    destruction!

Across the street from Rembrandt's house lived a scholarly
    rabbi,
    believing through sacred scripts that he was the Messiah.
In Rembrandt's portrait, the rabbi lives, a wise, melancholy
    man
    sentenced to the paradoxical destruction of learning.
All of us painters lust after disturbing, mystical presences.
    When I heard about the Rothko Chapel in Houston,
the space center city, I traveled there eagerly. Look! I
        thought
    this must be suicidal Rothko's challenge to Rembrandt's
    gray palette;
Rothko's black merging with red tones would conquer gray!

As I stared, I could not believe what I saw.
  Rothko, the great abstract impressionist,
master of lovely, floating color blocks,
  reds and blacks hovering, merging in space,
just before his suicide painted large, dark panels
  of contemplation for this chapel, panels overwhelmed
finally, completely by black, the tones of red hidden,
  as if the eye must accept black death
in order to find the final quietude of sight.

In Houston, where space and commerce turn and twist
  like desperate twins seeking both adventure and
    economic power,
I felt like the Flying Dutchman, a wanderer condemned to
  seeking
    lost connections. In this age of statistics, a so-called
      information age
focused on money, how could I return to New York to
  paint?
  New York, bursting apart with wealth against
    poverty,
art market like a crazy quilt of profit versus integrity,
  homeless in the streets like dirty bandages on blind eyes,
how could I go home to paint skeleton shadows?

(6) *Encounter with Van Gogh*

  Sauntering in dream along Amsterdam's peaceful canals under
a gray, Rembrandt sky, another spectre blocks my way. Van
Gogh insists: "We must paint in the sun to create bright colors,
not in this gray, murky atmosphere. Yellow, yellow is the true
sun's color!"

Rembrandt answers: "No! The force of color flows from the painter's eye piercing through dark weather. We draw not only from what we see, but from what we must see *through*!"

"*Through*, yes!" shouts Van Gogh. "We must paint *through*!"

"Through what?" asks Rembrandt, and they begin to laugh.

"Weather drains sight and paralyzes gray souls," Rembrandt continues. "The strong eye perceives weather as the soul's inevitable mask. If gray is the color of depression, it is also the color of the mind's edge where we live and discover fresh colors of meaning."

"Precisely!" argues Van Gogh. "My yellow is the color of the edge!"

"Gray!" insists Rembrandt, "with golden streaks!"

"Yellow!" cries Van Gogh, and they laugh again harmoniously.

(7) Rembrandt: Self-Portrait, 1652—46 Years Old

"Gesture is fixed to word,
    speaking beyond words
to voice their multiple meanings,
and achieve deathless forms
    that confront our death
and raise our vanishing anew.

"Here I show the middle years
    of life, past all return,
defiant questioner who has loved
and lost, who knows character is
    skeptical compassion of deep-set eyes
lustful to see, lustful to snare the viewer

"within lost, echoing forms of history.
    My life's purpose in this portrait

stares at the wonder of dramatic action;
see how I've lived, proud and stubborn,
     questioning the quick passage of time
with the dangerous, eternal passion of art."

(8) The Dutch Ghosts Continue Their Argument

"Yellow speaks to a time of madness," whispers Van Gogh under the gray sky. "You Americans appreciate the power of yellow. Seeking light, I had to free myself from Holland, from Rembrandt's dark paintings. I wanted to liberate color into astonishing sunlight! My aim was to portray a world dedicated to inflammatory colors, where line vanishes in feverish dots and slashes, a world proving light speeds into revelation! See today how my paintings spread throughout the world, contending even in this gray city with Rembrandt's museum!"

Rembrandt points to his *Jewish Bride*: "Yellow alone is madness! Yellow must be subdued in darkness where it turns to gold. See in my painting how man and woman await the time of union, the mystery of sexual discovery that is marriage. Golden with gobs of paint, the bridegroom's huge bent arm acts as a fulcrum to reveal a hand pressed to the bride's breast. Her fingers touch his hand tenderly in assent. Spectators cry in alarm at this intimacy! The triumph of sexual communion!"

Van Gogh laughs: "Once, I wrote, Rembrandt has alone, or almost alone amongst painters, a tenderness of expression. Your *Jewish Bride* is the tenderness I meant, expression without malice, without ironic observation. No sentimentality! Let gold emerge from dark to create phallus striking into cunt covered by the bride's right hand, her fingers spread, awaiting love's force soon to enter there. Alas, I could never paint this kind of sexual communion. All I could do was seek to free nature from Calvin's dark-colored, fanatic grip."

Yellow versus gold, Dutch spectres arguing in the clouds over Amsterdam. . . . *Expression without malice.* . . . Can I learn to paint without malice in this cynical age? In May 1890, five years before his suicide, Van Gogh painted as a tribute to Rembrandt, a *Raising of Lazarus*, all in yellow! Only Lazarus's shroud is white as he wakes from his death, astonished at the yellow-blazing world! . . . Today the forces of nature are revealed on an invisible, microscopic scale, creating new, magical, interior colors never seen before. . . . Inside our bodies, above us in endless space we have visions of vast, distant constellations. Is it ludicrous that I feel compelled to paint on a scale larger than Rembrandt and Van Gogh? I don't want to be confined to museums! I want to paint canvases for immense, communal spaces! I want the canvas to explode with the excitement of space voyages! And I want to restore dramatic faces and bodies to painting, human visions, sexual love, the intricate webs of power dreams! New risks that Rembrandt, Van Gogh, Rothko, Still, Diebenkorn, and Pollock would understand!

(9) *Rembrandt: Self-Portrait, 1669—63 Years Old*

"Echoes of time tell all, history is art,
colorful shadows create the mysteries
of ambiguity. The end has unexpected blessings
if art finds true survival forms.

"Every narrative speaks of radiant endurance,
worn-out skin legendary with achievement.
Death dies, leaving hope of resurrection,
since fading skin always seeks renewal.

"The true artist states passionately:
Style is not the man,
   style is the shaken forms of art,

forms that life creates enduring
   beyond time's battering changes.

"See how the paint's sacrificial spark
   reveals art's communal nature
      against man's defiant isolation!"

(10) *Departure*

Departing Amsterdam, in the train station
I see a cat raging in a wire cage, howling,
howling for escape to free, natural space.

How do I paint this wailing cat?

Rembrandt, you have taught me color
out of gray shadows, as you, Van Gogh, have helped me
perceive expression without malice exploding in yellow—

how to paint the wail, not just the agonized cat.

The wail reveals the questioning search
linking man to his animal nature; the wail
sounds through space, unconfined

by the cage's literal representation.
If I can paint the wail sounding
through the cat's confinement, perhaps

the Peaceable Kingdom will reign again,

when the cock crows for dawn's mysterious rise,
and natural skies rule with their transformations,
changing codes of intricate, fresh structures.

Painting is useless if it cannot build sanctuaries
against disorder, lightning ripples of discovery
against the tragic flow of life's ritual procession.

The world of vision has taught me how to rejoice
in great ancestors quarreling with us,
forcing us to reveal in art how we die to live.

SELECTED

POEMS

From *Private Dooms and*

Public Destinations:

Poems 1945–1962

The Will of Writing

The will of writing is
to make the pen
sound a word,
the sound neither hard nor soft,
but of that balance
which gives forth
something surrounded,
shining and stopped.

In the Peaceable Kingdom a Man Sings of Love

Sing the simple word as the word of love.
The word of love is a singular stare
disdaining the garden of satire.

Love's word is a light-charmed word,
belled and soft in the peeled glare
glowing above the hawkweeds of death.

When the angel began his descent to die,
he sang of love as the wisdom of quietness
winding on the spool of God's quiet eye.

Funeral

Four black suits led by a snout-beetle
      with down-curved beak
heaved in the coffin—that great, carved walnut weight—
on it a small wreath of roses.
The long-headed, low, black car
      swam in sultry light like a snake-bird
         down the street.
After the hearse, a procession of used cars
followed with relatives, dilly-dally,
with formal signs on their windows,
      FUNERAL.
I thought: in Japan, the festival of lanterns—
those huge, scampish shades with wanton colors—
      is for the souls of the dead.

A Plea for Alias

Coleridge, they say, lived in fantasy.
Under the name of Silas Tomkyn Comberbeck,
he enlisted in a regiment of dragoons.
I too like alias, a blaze of illumination:
    Bird of Paradise for Strelytzia—*Romanticism*
    Quail for Colinus Virginianus—*Classicism*
Alias I regard as a form of upper air;
when you live in the air of alias,
names fly free from their skins
like mail flying free from the dead letter box.
Alias of course has electric errors.
Once I knew a patriot who called his daughter
    University of Texas—*Naturalism*
U.T. we called her for shorthand,
Universal Tribulation said a secret friend.
Seldom do we find the right alias.
Young as Huck Finn we stuck our gum
on theatre seats where W. C. Fields played
Cuthbert J. Twilly and Larson E. Whipsnade.
But the quick grass of alias still grows
in the upper air if you strain your eyes—
Alias transmuting the common metals of life,
beating up elixirs, the golden alchemist.

A Guilty Father to His Daughter

Why are you always glad to me?
shouts my daughter gladfully
a twist of time a tuneful word
happy I roll into the glad gully

High Father in my Morning Glory
silk virtue violently in me
I rule my family like an old fox hound
and father my way in fancy

When I curse her she catcalls
and cancels her sparky consent
carnal her sun foams out and her flesh
firms between us fixed as cement

Prince of Fathers in my glad gully
hobbledehoy in my fatherly rain
why are you always glad to me?
Demon down the fatherly drain

Death of a Cat

A sultry summer evening, the children playing jacks
        in the hot and grimy garage
        under the yellow eyes of their gray cat,
        when the rubbery jack ball
        popped like a bubble into the street
and the cocky cat after its red-streaking path.

Brakes scrunched, the cat shot up like a spark,
        hit harshly over a tilted ear,
        and the cross-legged children screamed
        at the driven death of their pet.
        While I hauled a hose to clean
the clotted pavement stains, I thought of an ancient legend.

In the Irish Golden Age, three fasting clerks on pilgrimage
        sailed hungrily off to sea,
        praying with soft and folded hands
        their serene faith in God's care.
        But the young clerk said in his caution,
"I think I will take the silence of my small, gray cat."

On the rocky shore of an island, they beached the boat
        and kneeled to speak the Psalms;
        the cat crept to a wild wave
        and snatched a salmon from the foam.
        Still the clerks doubted the Lord's hand
until the fish began to burn on a sudden fire of coals.

Kneeling shadowy on the oily pavement, I saw
        some jelly of the cat's lost brain,
        a little mound of curious cells
        clinging against the asphalt road
        and fountainhead of lashing water.
Only the hose's full fury washed the cells away.

The myth of the supernal fishing claws grew old
        in the gray silence of evening,
        lost in the glittering air;
        though as water smashed the cells
        they flickered in tingling twilight
like sparks snapping through the foam of a fire.

Neighbors

Next door
in a shingle-sliding house
with paint curling off like worms
            in their crawling pace,
lives the neighbor whose guts I hate
            with his miser-face.

His house
is a jungle of mice and junk,
and he means to cut my property value
            with his ugly mess
of broken furniture, decaying wood,
            nothing to bless.

In the morning
he stakes out his property line
with a tall, imaginary fence;
            I feel barbed wire
though he only hammers sticks in the ground
            with eyes of fire.

His little head
sits on his neck like a grape,
and the rags of his clothes fill with dirt.
            To treat him mean
I give laughing parties for my friends.
            He watches behind a screen.

I think he was born
to live a hermit's isolation and serve
himself with trembling hands,
   trapped in a shell
of darkness where cold air blows
   no saving church bell.

   But every time
I look at him with hate he changes,
his shoulders sag and his head sinks.
   He decays with his house,
as I paint desperately to keep my house alive
   and set traps for any mouse.

The Momentary Glimpses of Women through Windows

At dusk time, the time of softness, I catch
a momentary glimpse of women through windows,
beautiful, strange, absolute.
I drive home to you through evening fog
flowing like the smooth sap of a varnish tree
over Christmas lights brilliant as scarlet fire birds
flying through old memories of desire.
Along the street the domes of evergreens
sing that women are like shade trees,
and the city traffic stares through smoke
with the sullen frenzy of ancestral strangers
searching for love through nets of circumstance.
I think of you waiting, my love, like these
momentary glimpses of women through windows,
beautiful, strange, absolute,
rays of wonder like the starfish on some foreign beach
whose distance measures only my desire coming to your waiting.

The Rake's Resentment of Verdi's *Falstaff*

A fat man, massive mercenary,
trapped by saint and shrew,
learns in the end lust must choke,
sings, *the world's a joke,*
white-bearded age as a Merry Andrew.
When lusting flesh ends its smoke,
laughter soars to the mercy seat
and sings out loud in any church pew—
old age can laugh when not in heat.

The Descent: Hotel Biron (The Rodin Museum)

"I remember now that in *The Imitation of Christ*, particularly in the third book, I once put sculpture everywhere in the place of God, and it was right and gave the right meaning."

Rodin, as quoted in Rilke's *The Rodin-Book*

Begin with line drawings, preparations,
parts of the body becoming purpose,
moving flesh fixed in naked vision.
Enter the stone, the descent begins:
chip and hammer, craze and caution,
the long suffering, shaping,
shadow of stone forms, elusive as mercury,
twisting before *The Gate of Hell,*
the sculptor of sexuality shaping
sex as a source, not a symbol.

"Je commence à comprendre," he mutters over and over;
always a beginning without end;
waiting, growing, as Rilke said,
Rodin's secretary of silence,
until the arch of a worn world
sings from the depth of stone,
sculpture in the place of God:
      Orpheus, crushed by his lyre,
      singing mutely out of the bronze;
      Christ embraced on the cross
      by the naked, clutching Magdalene;
      L'Eternelle Idole, man kneeling
      to kiss the belly of his eternal idol.

The Thinker thinks forever, thinking of passion,
the lover loves forever, fondling the thought,
opposition is the quest, the ore,
the surface ornament and orifice,
the eight arms of the octopus embracing the sea,
halved by the four arms of man and woman
who wake in the night to seek each other.

Stories of the Soviet Union: June 1961

(1) The Old Peasant Woman at
the Monastery of Zagorsk

Her face wrinkles out like tree rings in a cut-off stump.
Dirt lines her muddy, rigid veins.
Sighing, swaying to booming, battering bells,
she hunches on a bench beneath plane trees,
black kerchief tight around her graying head.
Starlings shoot like darts from golden onion towers;
a throaty choir chants within the cathedral
as the robed priest steps through a screen of ikons,
long, white beard foaming down his chest.
Through the courtyard, tourists chatter from a bus,
photographing Muzhiks from some lost grandmother's myth,
arguing happily, aimlessly, about horse-drawn days.
Their beards, tobacco-stained, bob in the sun
like buoys marking surface memories over the deep past.
Fluttering at a tourist, the withered face hisses,
"Kam-moon-eest?" "Nyet, Democrat." He shrinks
away, smiling, from dirt, as she pours over him
with kissing praise, a burning peasant face
in the path of power from Genghis Khan to Stalin.
Back she mutters to hunch on the bench in sun,
her silent fury of bones hammering the boards.

(2) The Lubyanka in Moscow

Dream of a Piranesi fortress,
caverns startled with mystical space
housing romantic prisoners with veins of fury?
The building used to be for life insurance.
It squats like any middle-class wall
ponderous for service, weighing money claims.
This way language dies, revolution hides;
evil of continuous interrogation earns
the name, *Conveyor Belt*, delirium
where ideal fantasy becomes a factory
manufacturing distorted mirrors,
confessions dissolving virtue to crime;
hallucination of error, like crushing snails,
nightmare crawling shells, where slime
of the "inner prison" seeps through complacent walls.

(3) The Lenin-Stalin Mausoleum in Red Square

> "I fear
>   the mausoleum
>   and official functions,
>   established statute
>   servility
>   may clog
>   with cloying unction
>   Lenin's simplicity."

Mayakovsky, *Vladimir Ilyich Lenin*

"How madly they leap, the gold hands of Spassky. . . ."
Blocks away
        Mayakovsky
            hardens in his statue,

straining to see the Kremlin clock
overhanging the mausoleum,
leaping, gold hands shaping the wild time of history.
Below the clock
                    a long line of gapers,
                                        thousands pacing daily,
enters the tomb
                    for the descent
                                        to death.
Red Square,
            formerly a market place
                                    known as "red,"
"A word whose earlier meaning connoted beauty,"
Now a tomb's market,
                        faced with red Ukrainian granite,
black and gray labradorite,
                            topped with a crown
of red Karelian porphyry;
                        solid, luxurious
                                        slabs of irony,
a Pharoah's pyramid
                    to venerate
                                the Worker's Will.
Outside
        two honor guards
                            stand motionless as gargoyles,
rifles riveted to thighs,
                        eyes blinking like illiterate signals.
An officer commands
                    silence
                            for the ceremony of worship.
Down,

down into cold,
                where time is frozen with corpses,
down,
        down,
                where light
                        lures into ice,
                                niches of idolatry.
In the depths
                two rigid guards
                        with fixed bayonets,
sharp points
        glittering through gloom
                        in threat of knives;
another officer,
                dead soul of an Inspector General
                        pinned to ribbons,
stares haughtily
                at the slow-snaking spectators.
There!
        the coffins,
                cold, mummy figures like wax,
chemistry of
        eternal death
                        hardening their veins,
lying with closed eyes
                in the painted stare of ikons:
Lenin's small figure,
                prow of forehead,
                                sensitive face,
aesthetic beard,
                a respected teacher's dignity
shining from suit and tie

                    beside his brother, Stalin,
whipmaster
                in tunic of power,
                            Roman uniform of conformity,
flowing mustache
                    like fur of a black bear,
coiling cave power in a coffin,
                        Dostoyevsky's Grand Inquisitor
whispering to his Christ:
                    "We have corrected Thy deed
and based it on Miracle,
                        Mystery,
                                and Authority
And men were delighted
                    to be led again
                            a herd,
and that
            there had been lifted
                        from their hearts
at last
        the terrible gift
                    of freedom. . . ."

Dazed,
        the emerging line
                    warms to sunlight
and stares
        at names of leaders
                    buried in the Kremlin Wall:
Zhdanov,
            Stalin's butcher of the arts,
                    demanding Socialist Realism;

Krupskaya,
		Lenin's wife,
				still protesting against
the cult of personality
				that embalms her husband
						as a God;
the missing shadow of Trotsky
				arguing vainly
in favor of the Revolution
				with the plea that it
"Leads humanity
			from the dark night
					of the circumscribed I";
while the faint,
			symbolic voice
				of Alexander Blok
whispers
		from his Scythian poem:
					"Russia is a sphinx.
In joy
	and grief
			and pouring with black blood,
she peers,
		peers,
			peers at you,
				with hatred
						and with love."

From Sword, Sex, and God's Word
at the Philosopher's Gate

Descartes Composes a Ballet

Death looks like my natural daughter
who died at the age of five; she dances
toward me in her skeleton; I cannot remember
her mother, though, long ago, it was a warm embrace.
Cold of death here in Stockholm. I rise
at five every morning to teach Queen Christina
in her study. She is killing me with arguments
of how to live happily in sight of God and man.
Always I yearned for morning hours in bed
and warmth for thought. In the Bavarian Army
during the Thirty Years War, I climbed in a stove
each ice-shattered morning to keep warm
and meditate. The Queen is my stove,
impatient youth, commanding mistress of logic.
With her I have analyzed love, and the Passions
of the Soul residing in the tiny pineal gland.
Her Majesty of Argument has set me to compose a ballet.
Skepticism dances toward my luring senses.
Am I sitting by this fire in my dressing gown?
Sometimes I dream I sit here quietly for warmth
when I am naked in bed. Madmen have such dreams,
but there remains something I cannot doubt.
No demon can deceive me if I do not exist.
Though I think everything false, I am
something since I think. . . .
Small defense against this passionate Queen

who walks in logical snow to freeze my age.
I have delved in matter and freed its substance
from the ancient world, but not from God.
Mind and matter are God's creatures, His will,
and hence distinct from Him. They dance
a singular science for which I went
on pilgrimage to the Blessed Virgin's shrine.
The dancers shall whirl in passion of faith
out of the sunlit south into this dark north.
God, being good, will not deceive their limbs.
If they stumble, it is her whirling will,
her will to death that kills me in this cold land.
Even if mind sleeps in my daughter and madmen,
God's mind will dance in this ballet
and the Queen see my dancers triumph over death.
Why should we marvel if the light reflected
from the body of a wolf into the eyes of sheep
excites them to quick flight? Mind is music,
God is beyond, God stands to Himself,
invisible dancer who dances quicksilver vision.

Rousseau Takes His Five Natural Children
to the Foundling Hospital

1

I search for a man in the integrity of Nature,
and this man shall be myself. I know my heart
and have studied mankind. Such as I was,
I declare myself, sometimes vile and despicable;
at other times virtuous, generous, and sublime.

2

My mistress was a needlewoman of good family.
Always a friend to decency in manners
and conversation, I took her part.
She saw in me an honest man, and I perceived
in her a simple heart, devoid of coquetry.

At first amusement was my only object;
then, I found I had given myself a companion.
I began by declaring to her shyness
that I would never abandon or marry her,
and so, we began to conceive bastards.

3

Too sincere and haughty in my inquiring mind,
I had to examine the destiny of my children
according to the laws of Nature, Justice, and Reason,
and those of that Religion, holy and eternal,
which men have polluted with purest desire.

I trembled to entrust them to their mother's family,
ill brought up, to be still worse educated.
In abandoning my children to public education
for want of the means of bringing them up,
I considered myself a member of the Republic of Plato.

4

Sometimes in the privacy of my study,
with my hands pressed tight over my eyes,
or in the darkness of the night,
I think that there is no God.
But I see the rising of the Sun,

as it scatters mists that cover the earth
and lays bare the wondrous, glittering
scene of Nature; my clouded soul clears,
I find my faith again, and my God,
and I prostrate myself in His natural world.

5

I have written the truth; whoever examines my character
and pronounces me dishonest, deserves the gibbet.
The noble, savage man, when he has dined
is at peace with all Nature; natural,
we sense the glad mystery of God.

Only by institutions is man made bad,
yet that is my fear of the Foundling Hospital.
The faces of my children I have never known
flare behind the walls of that gray school
and I see them, forever, at their education.

*Freud, Dying in London, Recalls the Smoke
of His Cigar Beginning to Sing*

"Double-flesh,
double-way;
  love is a bed
where angel-devils
lash and play.

"Double-warmth,
double-flame;
  love is the fury
to love and find
a single name."

In the smoke of my cigars, twenty a day,
I searched the roots of man's desire;
to bed at one in the morning
until the smoke began to sing.
I enjoyed my food, my meat,
in a city whose name I have forgotten.
Rooted in one house for forty-seven years,
I analyzed and wrote and watched six children
until the Nazis marched and the booted Commissar
asked me to sign a statement of gentle handling.
I insisted on adding the sentence:
"I can heartily recommend the Gestapo to anyone."
The cancer grows in my jaw like a separate life.
Krebs, meaning cancer and crabs; strange that I
who am fond of crabs should suffer from cancer.
A broadcast says: *This is the last war*.
Anyhow, it is my last war. The radium begins
to eat in and my world is what it was before—
an island of pain floating on a sea of indifference.
The stench . . . when my chow is brought to visit me,
she shrinks into a corner of the room.
I spend my hours lying near my study window
gazing at my flowers in the garden,
my superb almond tree, its pink blossoms
pouring beauty into the darkening world.
I never believed in a supernatural life;
this world of nature embraces everything.
Why, then, do I dream of religion,
and write of Moses in my final hours?
Man's helplessness remains, his father-longing.
The gods retain their three-fold task:
to exorcise the terrors of nature;

to reconcile the cruelty of death;
to make amends for all suffering and hate
the communal life of culture imposes on man.
In early centuries, men projected the Devil;
today, their guilt turns into physical pain.
Jews write to beg me not to tear from Moses,
in time of need, the legend of a Jewish hero;
but the truth must be sought. Moses blazes
in my imagination more than any other leader.
For three lonely September weeks in 1913,
I stood every day by Michelangelo's statue,
studying it, measuring it, sketching it,
until I captured the understanding for it:
Moses, angry at the dance of lust,
the sexual fury around the Golden Calf,
but mastering his passion for his cause,
protecting the Tables of the Law.
It is so logical. Moses was an Egyptian Prince,
not a Jew; Moses was the God who chose the Jews,
desiring to make them equal to Egyptians,
to give them one God of purity and power;
and so he marked them with the rite of circumcision,
and led them into a land of freedom.
In the end, he was murdered in rebellion
and that murder bred the hope for a Messiah
of retribution. Christianity, the son-religion,
replaced the ancient, Mosaic father-religion.

The little Egyptian statues on my desk begin to speak:
God, the Father, always walks on earth
until his sons unite to slay him.
What was it that surrealist artist said?

My cranium is reminiscent of a snail. . . .
I crawled slowly through the years
until the smoke of my cigar began to sing.
It is useless to go on. . . . Burn me,
place my ashes in a Grecian urn. . . .

"Double-flesh,
double-way;
  love is a bed
where angel-devils
lash and play.

"Double-warmth,
double-flame,
  love is the fury
to love and find
a single name."

From *The Stalingrad Elegies* (1964)

The Piano on the Street

You must be ruthless, Margaret.
Make your flesh judge for a change,
as ours does here. Forget the sentiments
of tradition and status. Art is no aristocrat.
Then your disappointment will be less.
Always you saw in me not just a husband
and lover, but a pianist. A piano
in Germany is a peculiar sound,
a prideful, percussive tone,
our battering rhythm and yearning melody;
so I can understand why you still
write thinking of me as a pianist,
when I will never play again.
The fact is my hands are ruined.
Frostbite. The small finger on my left hand is gone,
and three middle fingers of my right hand.
I hold my drinking cup with thumb and little finger.
The thing I do best with the little finger is shoot;
I carry my rifle with me all the time,
though I can't go on shooting forever.
Perhaps I can play the huntsman in *Der Freischütz*.
"*Gallows Humor*"

The other day a piano appeared in the street,
yes, in the street, just off Red Square,
a street of apartment houses blown up
to flush out snipers. Some soldiers felt sorry
for the piano and carried it out into the street

73

before the house flew into the air.
Every passing soldier hammered away at it
with one finger, folksongs, love songs,
nursery songs, explorations of the past.
Then Kurt Hahnke, you remember him
from the conservatory in 1937?—
(Everyone called him "promising,"
that cruel cliché, "a fine technique,
but a little cold; he lacks experience.")
Well, he played supremely well here this January.
A hundred soldiers squatted listening
in their heavy coats, dirty blankets
over their helmets and heads for warmth.
He played the *Appassionata* of Beethoven.
If I could only write you an analysis
of this sonata from a *military* point of view!
Remember when we heard Gieseking play it?
Fast and faster to the inevitable end.
Kurt played it even faster; you would
have called it *merciless*, we were
always too sentimental about music—
"Beethoven is beautiful." Yes, but what about
compulsion, brutality, frustration, rage?
Beethoven was Beethoven, sentenced to be a German too.
He understood Napoleon ("He is only
        a man after all, like any other.")
Just as Stalingrad understood Beethoven.
The first pianissimo, that falling and rising
F minor chord with the uncanny trill at the end
of the phrase, came whispering out of the snow.
You know I always hated literary comments
on music; I almost agreed with Goebbels

when he banned criticism of the arts;
but I think now words are much the same as notes,
each merges suggestion and detail in precise rhythm.
Remember, the *Appassionata* was only played
some twelve years after Beethoven's death.
The pianos of his *time* couldn't stand the *force*;
they were built for the tame elegance of salons.
They couldn't even sustain the slow melody of the *Andante*.
They were built for baroque ornaments and peering nymphs.
I know now what Beethoven's trills
in this sonata really mean, they are webs of enigma
out of which is spun, not resolution,
but endless transition, other turns, other keys.
The second movement is the only rest,
an absolute necessity for tranquillity and peace
between violence, compulsive pity,
and pitiful compulsion (do you understand the difference?).
For the first time I heard people really listening
to this movement. *There is no modulation in it,*
as if to say the lost harmony exists only
in one key, one purpose, one inner peace.
Then fury again, driving chords and syncopations,
at the end no liberation, no brotherhood,
merely strength and fortissimo pace to disaster.
This is the way to end, three quick chords,
three quick shots, three frozen fingers;
behind the music, the sound of distant artillery,
but everyone listens only to the exploding notes.
Streets, rubble listen, ears hang
on the skeleton walls, on bent, shot-out street lamps
as deafness finds its inner sound. . . .

The Snow Woman

Yesterday I made a woman
out of snow, made love to her,
        white breasts,
        white thighs.

Cold, perfect, pure,
shining in the night,
I shaped her to freeze
        beyond time.

She never spoke a word
of warmth as we made love,
yet her frozen tongue kissed
        beyond dream.

Her ice was my desire,
her white perfection
glittered in my eyes,
        white breasts,
        white thighs.

The Wound of Flatness

We live on the ruled edge of things.
The eye sees level, straight,
this damn country that never curves.
You dream of devils in white suits
heating up red wounds,
of marching, marching, till you fall off
the edge of Columbus' world.
I know the fantasies of mapmakers:
men who dream of curves,
women, worlds, wineglasses,
roundness that returns.

Everything that passes here
has a sense of flatness
and I must tell you
that I, too, am down.
I am in a field hospital
waiting transport home.
The date is always changed
on our frozen calendar.
We may wait forever.

You must know some time . . .
My legs were shot off
below the knee and thigh.
Next to me lies a mask
without a nose or arm.
"I'll never use any more

handkerchiefs," he says.
"What if you cry?" I joke.
"We won't have a chance to cry," he laughs,
"We're in the square world now for sure,
Mr. Flat Legs and Mr. Flat Nose."

I send you love from the earth's surface.
It is best if we never meet again.
You in your round world, I down here;
for my legs would always remember
loving you, encircling you,
walking with you, running to your roundness.

Sometimes I think of killing myself,
but I helped to make this world
and I'll live in it as long as I can,
like a chessman with a flat bottom
moved across a board to the edge.

From *Violence and Glory:*

Poems 1962–1968

Withered Daffodils

Although they droop in front of a city store
in the heat where weekend shoppers hustle,
I buy you dozens of fading, withered daffodils
for sharpened yellow shine of memory—
that day when mountain slopes began to burst
with sudden color, revealing graceful bells
of spring that burnished silence with a sudden
space of vision, a landscape for our love.
You take them in your hand, arrange them
in your vase where they stand, vulnerable,
crumbling into brown, dying symbols,
a gift of destruction that memory may
always burn with the visionary landscape
where body stretches eagerly, flesh reveals. . . .
You put on Mozart's *Requiem*. . . . Voices
sing the source of light, "In lux perpetua,"
the natural resurrection which our eyes absorb
from flowers and trees, though only love perceived
flashes that miracle of light in flesh.

London Pavement Artist

His place is before, not in, the National Gallery,
on the sidewalk, down on hands and knees,
gray hair a massive flag of identity,
hands like hooks grappling with stone,
savage beard a porcupine defense
against the jeers of passersby.
Draw to eat. Simple motivation,
but what eats him is the pavement,
devouring his images of chalk;
that rain-washed, fog-lost, wind-whipped cement
on which he draws flowers and faces,
simple subjects to elicit simple coins,
penny and ha'penny thudding in his cap.
Is it art? Stupid question.
The images of chalk fade in the rain. . . .
Art is the pavement that eats you.

After the Objects, a Subject

After the objects, meticulous, detailed,
portrayed with agonizing, aesthetic perfection,
fragments of ideal order devoid of place,
to see a subject, crazy, accidental,
edgy with pride of human absurdity.
I'm stopped at a tunnel near woods, underbrush;
a red sports car tuned to open space
drives up, parks; a tall man in brown cap
unwinds his legs somehow from the wheel.
Slowly he emerges, red vest, white,
buttoned sweater with a flashing silver
trumpet growing from the long fingers of his hand.
He strides with purpose into the bushes,
not to piss, but to blow, man, hit the highs
free from complaining neighbors cramped
in thin walls of tight apartment houses.
The sound glides and glistens in air
like a sharp knife cutting glitter of fish scales,
music in the lost woods returning
to the inevitable, natural subject.

The Clear Angels of Dawn in the Country

The clear angels of dawn assault the eye,
the temporary angels of dawn, naked
in light, transparent radiance that burns away
shadows of green trees, brown houses, blue bay.
The Great Blue Heron nesting in the redwood grove
fires the ancient thrust of green branches
with angelic altitudes, luminous flights
that alter the eye in dance of wings and air.
Even the solid house in early morning sits
a little lighter, rising out of beds
through windows, doors, into the fleshy trees,
the wooden angels flowing back to their source.

As for the garden, nothing grows, earth waits
a moment for the mastery of light, the oaks
sharpen their leaves for day's authority;
the dew evaporates in the sun's heat
where drying waterdrops reveal
angelic masks, wet and fragrant to the nose,
then gone, invisible, as green leaves deepen
in the sun's demands for light more powerful,
more certain than an angel's natural transparency.
Farewell, lost angels of the morning,
the harder images of day are clear, the dream
of dawn remains, those angels in that new air.

From *Ambiguous Dancers of Fame*

(1987)

Mexican Flower Arrangement

In a narrow waterglass
on the porch overlooking the sea
my wife has settled
a thick-stemmed red carnation
and a pale pink hibiscus
its petals and delicate white veins
flaring out in the ocean breeze,
the little yellow pollinating dots
on its long pistil stem
a singular flagpole of color
     for a common waterglass.

As the poet, Pellicer, says,
flowers and death are the Mexican dreams.
To these I add the waterglass
and the hands of feminine love
that arranged the flowers
permitting the fragile hibiscus
to flutter against blue sky
and relentless spindrift waves—
If I were a painter I would paint
this still life with the naked arms
of the woman arranging the flowers
     for love against time.

The Dreamer of Light Sings His Song of Sounds

When darkness lingers, enclosing tightly,
birds begin to sing the song of sounds,
tentative phrases that puzzle the air—
is there a complete sentence, a finished song?
The dreamer of light responds with dawn,
searching stories change to sunlit music,
melodies force blood through sleeping bodies
and the earth-chorus, led by the rooster,
challenges time to accept its beginning eye.
Look! see the past triumph with its ruins,
love-battles, poverty begging on sticks,
indifference of wealth, death whipping dogs
and horses, speeding his cars up the highway.
Only wait! the dreamer of light appears again
requesting once more the marvelous song.

Roadblock

When the army stops you
at a roadblock, no faces
loom in the dusk, only guns,
stance of uniforms,
inspection's casual look.
The guessing game begins,
who, what, is hiding there?
Searching hands caress,
invade your private space
as if death, laughing with glee,
hides in the smallest purse,
explodes in the exhaust.

Neighboring Walls

Not wealthy, but relatively "secure,"
"paying on a retirement plan,"
close to sixty and yearning for
Social Security, I find myself living
next to three families in two shacks.
We greet every day over the stone wall.
I hear their radio pound out religious pleas,
soap operas, Spanish songs of lost love.
I watch their many children play soccer,
play chewing gum, play sit-and-wait.
I see their old women, grandmothers,
chopping wood for the family stove,
cooking piles of tortillas, beans. . . .
I watch their youthful men set off
to work on roads for three dollars a day,
stagger home drunk on weekend fiestas,
grinning children leading them by the arms.
All of this I see and do not see
because of the thick stone wall between us
and I write this poem to peer over
walls that always rise to separate
social language from solitary song.

The Writer and the Gardener

I shut out his world; he shuts out mine.
To him plants, trees, grass are words.
To me words are plants, trees, grass.
Working at the typewriter I look out.
Working with a shovel he looks in.
We greet each other when we pass.
My world to him seems like a dream
of time that has lost its sense of place.
His world seems to me like a dream-garden
to forget the masks of poverty and race.
Yet without gardens how would we see?
And without words how would we change?
The gardener and I have made our truce.
Words and flowers bloom, fade as the wind blows.
I use a shovel, he writes with a rose.

The Gardener's Celebration

At seven in the morning on my birthday
while I'm asleep, he sets off a string
of red rockets under my window.
Then he brings in a bottle of whiskey,
a Pan Dulce, makes a pot of chocolate,
sits me down, dazed, to celebrate.
While my head still rocks with the rockets
he cuts the sweet bread, pours out chocolate,
and we drink the whiskey in morning sun
as birds sing and flowers glow through corn.
Look! A birthday means *birth*, I feel newborn!

The First Heavy Rain of the Rainy Season

Her face wrinkling deeply like the steep land,
the old Indian woman smiles her worn, balanced smile:
"For some of us the rain is good,
for some of us it's bad.
Those who plant by the lake
need no water, for them
this heavy rain is a danger.
Those who plant on the hills
welcome rain, for them
it is the force that saves.
In all things nature kills
and blesses; when those in the hills
know death, the valley thrives.
When those in the valley know death
the hills blossom with green corn.
We look from valley up to hills
and see the landscape of God
balanced like an ancient sword.
To celebrate the rainy season
we begin our sacred village dance
of balance between valley and hills.
That is why we have two cheeks, two arms,
two breasts, two eyes, two legs.
That is why we have man and wife,
to seek a difficult unity
and tie a golden string to heaven
that moon may seek dawn-light."

Dog-Pack

Mornings in the Sangre de Cristo mountains,
sun rising over Santa Fe below,
desert glowing red and green in dawnlight,
the dog-pack arrives to accompany us
through juniper and pine trees.
My dog expects them, waits eagerly,
barking at them in frenzied dog-language.
They put up a huge brown jackrabbit,
and race with spectacular failure
after his hopping body into a meadow
fragrant with yellow and white wildflowers.
Panting with frustration and satisfaction,
the great dog-pack returns slowly
after chasing the ardent American dream,
eyes shining with the pursuit of happiness
embedded in the central meaning of dog-pack.
Dog-pack knows how the natural community
decides finally how a civilization
leaves its individual traces on time,
not the isolated heart which dies alone.

Frank Lloyd Wright Desperately Designing a Chair

Sitting is an
unfortunate necessity.
Everyone knows
reclining is the
only attractive
posture of relaxation.
So I will not let you relax!
Let us all sit
straight at attention
enjoying the requirements
of eating and conversing.
With good talk
flowing into our ears,
we must not sag
or slump into disarray.
Between contempt and desperation
rises the vision
for designing a chair.
As you sit in my chair,
coming from the world of desperation,
on guard against contempt,
you encounter the
clear, sharp lines
of my design,
sit ramrod straight
with the angels of necessity.

The Oedipus Scream of Olivier

To trap a rare ermine
strew salt on the ice.
The ermine licks
that tantalizing taste,
his tongue freezes to the spot,
and Oedipus screams out
his incestuous guilt
as Olivier's performance
mimics the ermine's fate.
In such metaphors,
in such sharp memory shine
the grace of our struggle,
the force of our animal defeat
confronting invisible gods,
how silently they sit
waiting in some frozen pit.

All Day Driving across Kansas

The distance stretches
so far
you drag it
around after you,
no stopping lights,
no ending doors.
The highway engineer
says when you build a road
straight
there's never a return.

Love Song in Summer's Furnace Heat

Let the white blossoms blow,
my love is gone
and summer's furnace heat rolls on.

Let the white blossoms blow.
Hell lines the freeways
with fumes of foul days.

Let the white blossoms blow
telling when my love returns,
love learns when it burns.

From *The Complete American Fantasies* (1996)

Always We Walk through Unknown People

Always we walk through unknown people
guessing them; the click of meeting
steps lightly into passing; our guess
rides through curious air in a glance
or grimace, an elusive grin;
walking through faces, eyes, legs,
arms, nodding necks, similar veins.
A peculiar pulse plods through flesh,
pounding a rage of recognition:
That person I guess is somewhere me,
somehow I walk in his difference;
this meeting sometime is our parting. . . .
To guess him is our only greeting.

The Country Fair of Childhood

Recall the country fair, memory,
rough canvas tents stinking of manure,
bright painted clowns laughing in
evening lights, lights soft as silk.
In holiday clothes the town arrives,
acrobats leap, the ringmaster stands
in limelight stance, rope hands of rule,
voice thick and lush as Panama.

Return, cries the country crowd, return,
flowing through popcorn and palmistry,
through cunning sideshow barkers
who know the whiskey spirit's spiny ways.
Return, cry my lost childhood friends,
through comic horror of freaks,
the fluffy fat lady rolling her flesh,
sword swallower, tinkling thin man,
those lost oracles of the pythoness.

Return, oh return to the dumb show's
ascension of awe and love holding
within its glow our circus rhythm.
These, our tents, we have raised not for
the splintered eyes of confessed faces,
but to celebrate the Big Sky's lusty cover.

Hats and Ears for Charles Ives

I want to make a music with its own ears.
Let the ears remain inconspicuous, at attention,
sounds penetrating through them into the body's flesh
causing the brain to glow burnished with detailed music.
The ears, the ears, from hearing comes soul-knowledge.

The ears of New England sing a joyous peace
remembering the pleasure of Sunday's raucous noise,
my father in his bright bandmaster's uniform
playing "Jerusalem the Golden" in the town square
while on neighboring roofs and verandas,

musicians answered with contrapuntal variations,
the echoes combining bold secular and sacred worlds,
uniting a country of democratic promise and desire,
a wilderness land awaiting the immigration rush
that pushed feverish America into ethnic competition.

Growing up in Danbury, a hatters' town,
families worked at home at their own pace,
shaping practical cover as well as hats of pride;
then simple hatters turned into Hat Manufacturers
and factories grew with masks of anonymous labor.

The town burst into banks, Savings Companies,
messages of insurance invaded my head.
I made my wealth by selling life insurance,

seeking to make it a beneficial science by
showing men the statistical nature of security.

What I began is now called "Programming"
or "Estate Planning," figures as machine thought.
My mind full of Emersonian optimism, I wrote:
"As the raindrops falling together make the Rivers,
so men seek common life together for a season. . . ."

Discovering that politicians mired in pride are
the chief cause of war, my mind moved to social democracy.
As politicians defend the nature of large properties,
is not the fighting done by men of little property?
Thus property becomes the red axe of division.

In my lost Danbury town I danced with the group,
music and hats as the colorful, measured ceremony,
but in New York condemned to the isolation of size,
after work or weekends, I wrote endless notes on paper
that I could hear only in the sound of my sharp imagination.

Such sounds are heard by animals in cages,
listening vainly for a glory of space through bars.
Great minds hang in isolation like vultures
circling above lost unity with fixed dreams,
lustful country buzzards above decorous masquerades.

In the concert hall, I sit quietly dreaming music and hats.
When they boo my music I sit like a rigid patrician,
but if someone boos the music of my friend, Ruggles,
I shout: "You goddarn, sissy-eared mollycoddle,
stand up and use your ears like a man!"

Like Emerson I wish to be an invader of the unknown.
Is not music like an insect buzzing, whirring?
Can it not strike like a clear bell or distant thunder?
In my old age I wear a broadbrimmed campaign hat
to preserve the ears and hats that make a country dream.

Wallace Stevens at Ease with Marble Cake

Last weekend I spent the afternoons
sitting in my garden at home,
at ease in a solitary situation.
I drank a glass of White Burgundy
and watched my neighbor's pigeons.
A black and white is an old friend
I call Marble Cake. Sitting near him
with a little Kraft's Limburger Spread,
pouring myself a second glass of decent wine,
that big, fat Marble Cake moves around,
strutting, keeping his sharp eye on me,
doing queer things to keep me awake.
Marble Cake, my fat Pigeon Master,
teaching me the drift of imagination at ease,
how the grace of sound reflects
a still point in time dancing in the light,
where imagination reveals its proud presence
transforming the commonplace into points of brilliance.

The Peaceable Kingdom of Edward Hicks

When the heart leaps in a world of wonder
where lion and deer wander together,
hope shines like a star of charity
and peace sings from the clear weather.

No time can be killed or wasted,
hands of love move the hours and days.
The lost animals rove home with joy
to a rich election that houses the strays.

Laughter from the eternal world sounds
as God blesses each animal's eyes;
bright, ascending acts of compassion
dazzle the dark surrounding lies.

Simple kingdoms soar in true reality
through the mind stunned by desire,
drive toward the sun the ideas of light
where meet the words and acts of fire.

Mr. and Mrs. Herman Melville at Home, Isolated in Their Rooms

"Herman has taken to writing poetry,
you need not tell anyone,
for you know how such things get around,"
his wife writes to a friend. . . .
She is sitting in her bedroom
across from his study, worried about him.
He has taken to closing his door,
shutting himself up, writing obscure poems,
a great manhole of isolation
with a peculiar, concealed look
that marks the losers of fantasy.
Some scholars laugh at her cautious words,
some guess frustrations of sex, religion,
a somber, puritanical heritage, decorous duty
masking, controlling the crawling visions. . . .
Perhaps she also feels poetry is dangerous,
a possibility. . . . Does she fear insanity
closing the door, tense in his study,
writing his labored, difficult poems?
They are still there, sitting in history,
wife and husband together, apart,
disciplined boarders pursuing separate lives
in visionary, secluded rooms,
worrying that poetry is
the shining grace of eternal language—
that we write only to preserve
a myth of words opposed
to the acts of love.

Huck Finn at Ninety, Dying
in a Chicago Boardinghouse Room

Give up everything and
float away under the sun!
The bliss of a bastard
cut off from everyone!

Feel your Moms and Aunts
pop their corsets like balloons,
and the breasts of love
soar out in white moons.

I sink back, a whiskey case,
fondling the button I found—
"Make Love—Not War"—
in the park on the ground.

I've got the button, button—
Let me sleep in the gleam
of that old raft floating downriver
through the frontier dream.

Bashir Was My Name

In 1962 when Lyndon B. Johnson was vice-president,
he met the Pakistani camel-driver, Bashir, and invited
him to the United States

Years ago that vice-president came,
singled me out from a crowd in Karachi,
and invited me to visit the United States.
I arrived at a winged place called
strangely Idlewild, flew to Texas
with my honorable host, rode his horses,
sampled his barbecue, visited the Dallas State Fair.
A few days later in Washington, I met the president
and said, "Now I have seen the Man of the World!"
Returning to my home I asked, "Can you live
in the darkness when a star sits on your shoulder?"
My shoulder began to hurt and gleam in the dark,
my son took over my camel cart.
In a friend's garage glows the pick-up truck
I was given in America. I am taking driving lessons.
When I get my trucking permit, I will double
our family income. I have been received by
President Ayub Khan, feted by the American ambassador,
and had a standing ovation at the Lahore Horse Show.
Every night I go home to my house
across the railroad tracks in Bashir Chowk.
The old woman who sells cattle fodder,
the milk man whose water buffalos squat
outside my hut, and the betel nut vendor
come together to see my privileged possessions.
From under the single rope-bed in the hut,

I pull out the bag I took to America and show them
the awards of my trip through the sky:
a transistor radio, a Polaroid camera,
a PT boat pin, the badge of a Texas deputy sheriff,
a medal showing the City Hall in Kansas City,
a doll, half a dozen ball-point pens marked
"Compliments of the Vice-President of the United States."
And then I can sleep, or rather I dream:

"Once we were chosen. Chance
scratched us with claws,
marked us forever with a white
shoulder glittering beyond laws.

"Cursed, blessed with a white shoulder,
we dance into the dark,
and you can tell the dancers in the dance
by the gleam of that white mark."

On the Burning of Mingus's Bass

> Charles Mingus, virtuoso bass player and one of the giants of
> modern jazz, was evicted from his studio in New York on
> Thanksgiving Eve in a hassle with the city and the landlord. . . .
> The city marshal shouted at Mingus, "I'll make all your trash into
> garbage" and that is what was done. Mingus's piano was shoved
> downstairs, his bass hauled off to the sanitation department and
> burned, and most of his belongings have disappeared also. . . .
>
> > Ralph Gleason,
> > *San Francisco Chronicle*, December 7, 1966

When a wood mountain burns,
the high-level sense falls,
the tall, striding rhythm,
      thump-thump plucking
      of heat-strings,
that hot, holding tension,
      hearthstone of sound,
      smolder into silence.

In the crazy stillness, searchers
      hunt wild wood;
a scarred fear hides
      in sanitary fire;
the high joy,
      gut-peaks,
fade, lost in garbage
      in sullen quiet.

The burned silence
      glows flat
with no thumping size.

What Are the Most Unusual Things
You Find in Garbage Cans?

(A journalist questions members of the Scavengers'
Protective Association Inc. in San Francisco.)

Burristrezzi

After a wedding or baby shower
        I find
lots of gifts in the garbage.
What you don't like you throw away,
        I guess.
Sell it, you're a cheapskate,
  give it, you feel guilty,
     so you chuck it in the garbage.

Duckmann

Bikes, baby cribs, brand new coats.
Big hotels are the best for clothing.
Family districts you don't see nothing
too unusual. Lots of little stuff
but hotels you hold your breath for
       chuck-offs.
People buy too much and stagger out,
       loaded.
They don't have no camels nowadays,
and planes don't carry all that stuff.
My dog sleeps in the baby crib.

Benson

In the trash
behind the old Hall of Justice
once
      I found a wooden leg.

Jones

Plenty of girly pictures
      you know, gals
      stacked up to the sky;
you see one of them
      comin' at you
        in real life,
you'd take off
      zoom
      like a rocket.
But in a garbage can
      they don't smell so real.

Ferrore

I've found helmets, medals, a bayonet
for my World War I collection. The bayonet's
the first kind they made where you stick it in,
twist, and it don't come out without
bringing half a guy's insides with it.
I like to take a war in the past.
The uniforms were more colorful;
to wear those helmets you musta
had a head as strong as a rock.
When you got a medal, they strung it
real fruitcake on a rainbow ribbon.
You didn't just load your chest with
little bars and flags like now.

Hanford

Picture frames. Pictures too, sometimes,
landscapes mostly, cows, trees.
Once I found a picture of Jesus Christ.
I've got thirty picture frames at home,
all kinds of frames from plain to fancy.
I haven't bought one since I married.
Sometimes I just put 'em on the wall.
When there's nothing in the frame,
you can see the frame real good.

Painter

Cash
    wristwatches
      and a gold
        wedding ring

Swinton

I've got about twenty radios I found
all around my house, on the floor,
    on the shelves, in closets,
      on the bureau.

That way I make my own stereo.
Maybe I turn on four at the same time,
    or listen to different shows
      in different rooms.

News for breakfast in the kitchen,
music in the bathroom, baseball
    in the backyard with a beer,
      politicians in the basement.

Sometimes I just turn 'em all off
and walk around quiet through the rooms.
    That's a good feeling too,
      looking at all those radios.

Hamilton

Old books
    you never saw
        so many
            goddamn
                old books
                    with weird titles
                        like
"Rebecca of Sunnybrook Farm."

Bindini

The most unusual thing I ever found was
        an Espresso machine.
It worked and I still use it in my home.
        Every morning with that coffee
        and you've got the stomach
                for a day with garbage.

Kristallnacht

In my mid-forties, ruled by the curves and
angles of experience, straight lines fading,
I sit in a cheap, dirty apartment
in San Francisco's Fillmore District,
separated from my wife and children,
and listen to bottles tossed, tinkling
on the street, drunken escapes from poverty,
street of gray pigeons and dogshit,
newspapers sodden in the gutters.
Tomorrow I will walk carefully
through shattered glass, remembering
a cool fall day in Germany, November 1938,
when I visited a friend in Freiburg,
small, proper intellectual town,
where citizens cleaned their front walks
carefully, even in rain. Ancient Gothic
cathedral and famous medieval university,
Heidegger, the philosopher-professor there,
Das Nichts nichtet—Nothing nothingizes,
a philosopher mute amidst Nazi power. . . .
Kristallnacht, all over Germany that night
the Nazis smashed, looted Jewish stores.
In Freiburg they burned the synagogue and
built a fence in darkness to hide destruction.
A naive, young American music student,
I wrote my first poem about that burning.
I spent that night in a cheap hotel,
turning, turning on a lumpy mattress

beneath the soft cloud of a featherbed,
listening through the thin partition
to a Nazi stormtrooper screw a whore
on percussion springs. . . . Since then,
in many foreign rooms, I have heard
lives tinkle on cracked pavements:
a childhood friend in fast cars
smashing ruthlessly and smashed;
a teacher, intellectual suicide,
crazed between the tension of ideas;
a mother, proud, crippled, blind
in the rolling wheelchair of age;
friends, relatives, summoned to mystery
and violence when the peaceful air
splits with fragments of suffering.
Nights I wake, sweating,
Kristallnacht splinters in the cutting dark,
glass lives shatter from unnatural trees.

Green Frog at Roadstead, Wisconsin

Consider the way of a pleasant path,
walking through white birch, fir,
and spruce on a linestone trail
through quiet, complacent time of summer
when, suddenly, the frog jumps!
And you jump after him, laughing,
hopping, frog and woman, to show
the stationary world its flat ways.
Love is a frog, I grin that greenly
to your green eyes and they leap
at me. Up, I will enter the Frog World
with you and try the leaping ways
of the heart that we do not fail to find
the sunlit air full of leaping chances!

Love, Do Not Shun the Dark Gargoyle

That lost time which celebrated beauty
of the Virgin beyond corruption of flesh;
which awarded to loyal, sheltered ladies
heroic knights and legends of purity,
built carefully into the light of grace
these dark gargoyles, demonic rainspouts
protecting walls, saving worship
by drinking storms with bestial ferocity.
When salvation lights fade at evening,
beauty of flesh is swift to die
unless we feel the terror of weight,
the ugly endurance that anchors us
in drifting time. Love, in our celebration,
do not shun the dark gargoyle,
weird face glowing in proud perception,
wings chained to high walls,
who carries rain, like love,
free from the cold stones of time.

The Mathematician Thinking of Ghost Numbers

People count themselves into oblivion
where names lie numberless in death.
Old, they count backwards with every breath.
Young, they rock the walls toward twenty-one.
Numbers cannot tell the names of time.

Favorite numbers fade in meaning
as Buddha's father summoned forty thousand
dancing girls to keep his son's great spirit
attached to the world. Why forty thousand?
Numbers cannot tell the names of time.

Beyond three hundred lurks the world of chaos.
Two is comfortable, four summons
wild winds to attack easy success.
Climbing to thirteen is a laughing risk.
Numbers cannot tell the names of time.

Men of power invent fanatic numbers
that march and kill in hidden camps.
The trinity reminds us of a living hell
while the Maya zero puzzles as peaceful shell.
Numbers cannot tell the names of time.

On the Beach Watched by a Sea Gull

December storm briefly suspended,
ice melting, still air alert for sound,
I burn papers on the lonely beach
strewn with oil-soaked stones and garbage,
oil companies leaking money on the shore.
Behind me, a watcher is watching me,
a fat, tough sea gull, a strutter,
mouth clamped on a long silver fish.
Refusing to release his greed, he can't take off,
so he glares at me. Teasing him, I move closer,
curiosity down the slide to scorn.
Clutching his fish, he waddles indignantly away,
paddles through greasy water to a rock
ten yards offshore to show his scorn
and preserve his meal, frustrated that he
can't fly, eat, mock me from the air at once.
I almost throw a rock to scare him,
but restrain myself, spectator to his greed.
Forced to eat, he sucks the big fish down his throat
like a vacuum pump turned high to emergency;
then takes off, ringing the air with shrill anger,
flying around me in a fury of joyous delight
at eating his fish and having his flight too.
After the burning, I tell my wife about the gull's rage.
She shrugs: "You gave him indigestion. Was that nice?"
Eye-driven are the ways of compulsive watchers
who stare and find in visionary questions,
enigmatic answers disguised as burning action.

A Screamer Discusses Methods of Screaming

We all scream, most of us inside.
Outside is another world.
A neighbor fills her television dinner
with too much pepper and screams.
One woman stabs her door with a sword.
Another, overweight, steps in the shower
and screams, "Fat! Fat! Fat!"
A man who takes flying lessons
soars high in the clouds to scream.
Another dives to the bottom of his pool
where his screams bubble away underwater.
A friend cleans his gun, screaming, "Assassin!"
I like an interior, smiling scream.
When you walk past me on the street
I nod my head to you and, smiling, scream.
You never hear me through the smile.
The inside scream has no echo.

Street Corner Signals

Punctually, every evening in commuter traffic,
the broad-hipped Mexican boy sways on the corner,
eyes closed, dancing feet churning in tennis shoes,
ears tuned to joyous, invisible signals.
Bored commuters call him "mentally defective,"
cagey drivers, media-minded, say he's a Martian.
If the intense signals can never be decoded,
they transform his fat, placid flesh
into some heart-sucking, frenzied magnet
pulling steel filings through his skin.
No, the traffic's magnetized, not the boy,
who hears his chest full of singing birds.

William Carlos Williams and
T. S. Eliot Dancing over London Bridge
in the Arizona Desert at Lake Havasu

Come dance with me, Tom,
an American first name, friendly antagonists'
dance of ghosts, Bill Williams and Tom Eliot.
Give up the formal crust of your T. S.
Come dance with me naked
in front of the mocking American mirror
as I danced naked, lonely, joyous, in my room.
We dance over your Mississippi together
toward Arizona to see your London Bridge.
It isn't falling down into your Wasteland.
We numbered the huge blocks of Victorian stone,
dismantled the green Art Nouveau lamps,
eliminated the foggy Thames River atmosphere,
engineered every detail to dry Arizona desert
and resurrected her over a man-made lake.
Even your British mayor came to dedicate her anew,
American and British flags flying in unity,
drooping a little in one hundred and ten degrees
over Tudor buildings looming as facades of desert shacks.

All of the spectres you fled, Tom,
applaud this real estate promotion:
P. T. Barnum, Melville's Confidence Man,
The Lost Tycoons, Anderson's Winesburg grotesques,
Mark Twain's rubes and hicks, your mother
trapped in St. Louis, dedicated to Savonarola,
they all burst clapping out of their graves

to celebrate this bold, new grotesque frontier.
Listen, how they applaud imported culture for the cactus!

Come dance with me along the burning bridge, Tom,
as the hot pavement burns our naked feet
and we hop, singing, "Tom's home again!"
Our new community will cook us a barbecue
to celebrate the struggle for its desert identity.
Let's sit down and have a drink, Tom,
and relish our American concept of *grotesque*,
this town crying with evangelical fervor,
writhing with desire for lost historical connections.

Sit down, Tom, and revel in our American Grotesque,
our hidden voices cracking against your British tongue:
"Grotesque is the vulnerable, pathetic fantasies
we create in our joyous pursuit of love and property.
Grotesque is the mystery we eliminate to create
the sad, literal facts and buildings that desire mystery.
Grotesque is what we become when we seclude ourselves
in locked suburban communities closed to awe and wonder.
American Grotesque, sad, searching patron of beauty,
struggles to balance the comic weight of our fantasies
that glow in the sky with their singular distortions."